The Right Start to the Chinese New Year

Celebrate with 40 Recipes

By

Angel Burns

♥♪♥♪♥♥♪♪♥♪♥♪♥♥♪♪♥♪♥♥♪♥♥♪♪♥♪

License Notices

Get Your Daily Deals Here!

Free books on me! Subscribe now to receive free and discounted books directly to your email. This means you will always have choices of your next book from the comfort of your own home and a reminder email will pop up a few days beforehand, so you never miss out! Every day, free books will make their way into your inbox and all you need to do is choose what you want.

What could be better than that?

Fill out the box below to get started on this amazing offer and start receiving your daily deals right away!

SUBSCRIBE
—— TO NEWSLETTER——

Enter your email address ✉

https://angel-burns.gr8.com

Table of Contents

Chinese New Year Food Recipes

HHHHHHHHHHHHHHHHHHHHHHHHHHHHHHHHHHHHHHH

Chapter I – Appetizer Recipes

HHHHHHHHHHHHHHHHHHHHHHHHHHHHHHHHHHHHH

Recipe 1: Vegetable Spring Rolls

February 16th is Chinese New Year, and this year it's the Year of the Dog, a symbol of honesty and loyalty.

Makes: 4

Preparation Time: 20mins

Cook Time: 30mins

Total Cook Time: 50mins

Ingredient List:

- Cooking oil (for frying)
- 2 cloves garlic (finely minced)
- 1 stalk green onions (finely chopped)
- 8 shiitake mushroom caps (julienned)
- 3 cups cabbage (shredded)
- 2 medium carrots (julienned)
- 8 ounces bamboo shoots
- 2 handfuls bean sprouts (fresh)
- 2 teaspoons fresh ginger (grated)
- 1 tablespoon low sodium soy sauce
- 1 teaspoon dark sesame oil
- 1 tablespoon cornstarch
- 50 spring roll wrappers (defrosted)

HHHHHHHHHHHHHHHHHHHHHHHHHHHHHHHHHHHHHH

Instructions:

1. In a wok, swirl 1 tablespoon of cooking oil. On moderately high heat, add the garlic and green onion, frequently stirring.

2. Once the heat is sufficiently hot, add the mushrooms along with the cabbage, carrots and bamboo shoots.

3. Increase the heat to high and stir fry the veggies for 2 minutes, and then toss in the bean sprouts and ginger. Add the soy sauce followed by the sesame oil and cook for 60 seconds.

4. Spread the filling out onto a large cookies sheet, propping the sheet up on one side to allow any oil or sauce to collect in the bottom, and discard.

5. In a bowl, whisk the cornstarch together with ¼ cup of cool water, and stir to combine.

6. Place a spring roll wrapper on a clean and even working surface, and add 1 tablespoon of the veggie mixture to the corner of the wrapper. Carefully, roll the edge of the spring roll wrapper to enclose the mixture securely.

7. Fold the 2 side corners towards the center of the wrapper while continuing to roll. Dampen the top edge with the cornstarch-water mixture and tightly wrap the rest of the way, while making sure that the edges are sealed tightly. Place seam side facing down and cover with kitchen wrap as this will prevent them from drying out until you are ready to fry.

8. Gently slide, in batches, the egg rolls into the hot oil and cook for between 2-3 minutes, turning them over 2-3 times, or until the spring roll wrappers are golden.

9. Remove the spring rolls to a wire baking rack to drain.

10. Serve hot.

Recipe 2: Pork Dumplings

Chinese dumplings are one of the most popular Chinese New Year appetizers.

Makes: 6-8

Preparation Time: 20mins

Cook Time: 1hour

Total Cook Time: 1hour 20mins

Ingredient List:

- 1 tablespoon seasoned rice vinegar
- ½ cup soy sauce
- 1 tablespoon sesame seeds
- 1 tablespoon Chinese chives (finely chopped)
- 1 teaspoon Asian hot sauce
- 1 pound ground pork
- 3 garlic cloves (peeled, minced)
- 1 medium egg (beaten)
- 2 tablespoons Chinese chives (finely chopped)
- 2 tablespoons soy sauce
- ½ tablespoons sesame oil
- 1 tablespoon fresh ginger (minced)
- 50 dumpling wrappers
- 1 cup vegetable oil (for frying)
- 1 quart water

HHHHHHHHHHHHHHHHHHHHHHHHHHHHHHHHHHHHHH

Instructions:

1. Combine the rice vinegar with the soy sauce, sesame seeds, 1 tablespoon chives, and hot sauce in a bowl and put to one side.

2. In another bowl, combine the pork with the garlic, egg, 2 tablespoons Chinese chives, soy sauce, sesame oil and minced ginger and mix until incorporated.

3. Arrange the dumpling wrappers on a lightly floured, clean work surface and using a tablespoon, spoon the filling into the center of each wrapper.

4. Using your little finger, dampen and crimp the edge of the wrapper with a drop of water to seal the dumpling by making small pleats. Repeat the process until all of the dumpling wrappers and pork filling are used.

5. In a large frying pan or skillet over moderate to high heat, heat 1-2 tablespoons of vegetable oil.

6. Add 8-10 dumplings to the pan and cook for 2 minutes each side, or until browned.

7. Add 1 cup of water, cover and cook for 5 minutes, or until the pork is cooked through and the dumplings are tender.

8. Repeat the process with the remaining dumplings.

9. Serve with the soy sauce mixture and use as a dip.

Recipe 3: Crispy Seaweed

You can serve this crispy seaweed alongside appetizers including spring rolls, wantons, and spare ribs.

Makes: 4

Preparation Time: 5mins

Cook Time: 10mins

Total Cook Time: 15mins

Ingredient List:

- ⅓ cup + 1 tablespoon rapeseed oil (for frying)
- 10½ ounces kale (washed, dried, finely sliced)
- ½ teaspoons Chinese 5-spice seasoning
- ½ teaspoons sugar
- ¼ teaspoons sea salt

HHHHHHHHHHHHHHHHHHHHHHHHHHHHHHHHHHHHH

Instructions:

1. Heat the rapeseed oil in a wok over high heat.

2. Add ¼ of the finely sliced kale to the wok, and deep fry, while tilting the wok, for 1-2 minutes. The kale should be crispy.

3. Using a slotted spoon, remove the kale from the wok and thoroughly dry using kitchen paper. Repeat until all the kale is used.

4. Remove the wok from the heat. Pour out any of the excess oil from the wok.

5. Return the crispy kale to the wok, sprinkle with 5-spice seasoning, sugar, and salt.

6. Toss to combine, and serve warm.

Recipe 4: Bak Kwa – Chinese Pork Jerky

Thin pork jerky with five spice seasoning is a given for Chinese New Year. We bet though, once you've made it once, you'll be whipping up a batch all year long.

Makes: 15 (2 slices)

Preparation Time: 45mins

Cook Time: 50mins*

Total Cook Time: 9hours 35mins

Ingredient List:

- 2 pounds ground pork (minimum 20% fat)
- 2 tablespoons Shaoxing wine
- 1 tablespoon fish sauce
- 1 tablespoon dark soy sauce
- ½ teaspoons ground pepper
- 1 teaspoon sesame oil
- ½ teaspoons Chinese 5-spice seasoning
- ⅔ cup sugar

HHHHHHHHHHHHHHHHHHHHHHHHHHHHHHHHHHHH

Instructions:

1. Combine the pork, wine, fish sauce, soy sauce, pepper, sesame oil, 5-spice seasoning, and sugar in a mixing bowl and mix thoroughly for a few minutes. Cover the bowl and transfer to the fridge, overnight.

2. Prepare 5 sheets of parchment 15½ x10½" wide.

3. Using a blunt kitchen knife thinly spread a layer of the pork mixture onto each sheet of the paper leaving a 1" clear border.

4. Place a large sheet of kitchen wrap over the meat and with a rolling pin, smooth and roll the meat, to spread and even. Take the plastic wrap off and repeat until the meat is all used.

5. Place the sheets of meat on jelly roll style pans and bake in the oven at 250 degrees F for 15 minutes. The meat should be dry, so if it's a little oozy, pat it dry with kitchen paper. Allow to cool.

6. Slice each sheet of jerky into 6 portions.

7. Increase the temperature of the oven to 425 degrees F.

8. Place the meat and parchment paper on a broiler pan and grill for 4-5 minutes, making sure that the meat doesn't burn.

9. Take out of the oven, and using kitchen tongs, flip over.

10. Put the pan back in the oven for 4-5 more minutes.

11. Remove and allow to cool on a wire baking rack.

*Cooking time = 25 minutes for each batch of 2.

Recipe 5: Szechuan Pork Wontons

Easy to make pork-filled wontons in a spicy Sichuan red chili oil sauce

Makes: 8

Preparation Time: 30mins

Cook Time: 30mins

Total Cook Time: 1hour

Ingredient List:

- 1½ pounds ground pork
- 3 tablespoons cornstarch
- 2 tablespoons dry sherry
- 2 tablespoons light soy sauce
- 1 tablespoon Chinese rice wine
- 4 cloves garlic (peeled, minced)
- 1 (4") piece of ginger (peeled, minced)
- 40 (3½") square wonton wrappers
- 1 medium egg (beaten)
- Kosher salt
- 2 tablespoons Chinkiang black vinegar
- ½ cup Sichuan red chili oil

HHHHHHHHHHHHHHHHHHHHHHHHHHHHHHHHHHHHHH

Instructions:

1. Add the pork, cornstarch, dry sherry, soy sauce, rice wine, garlic and minced ginger in a mixing bowl.

2. Working with only one wrapper at a time, add ½ teaspoon of filling to the middle, lightly brush the edges with beaten egg and gently fold in half to form a triangle; overlapping opposite corners, and sealing together with egg wash. Repeat the process with the remaining wonton wrappers and pork filling until. Set to one side.

3. In a large pot of boiling salted water, cook the wontons, for 5-7 minutes, until firm and cooked through. You will need to do this in batches.

4. Take a slotted spoon and transfer the wontons to kitchen paper towels to drain, and place in a large bowl.

5. Season well with salt and toss with vinegar and red chili oil and serve.

Recipe 6: Chili Pork Spare Ribs

Feast on these succulent spare ribs. They're finger-lickin'
good!

Makes: 4

Preparation Time: 10mins

Cook Time: 1hour 30mins

Total Cook Time: 1hour 40mins

Ingredient List:

- 2½ cups groundnut oil
- 2 pounds pork spare ribs (split into individual ribs)
- 3½ cups chicken stock
- 1 tablespoon granulated sugar
- 2 tablespoons chili bean sauce
- ⅓ cup Shaoxing wine
- 2 tablespoons light soy sauce
- 1½ tablespoons dark soy sauce
- 2 garlic cloves (peeled, finely chopped)
- 2 spring onions (finely chopped)
- 3 tablespoons hoisin sauce
- 2 tablespoons yellow bean sauce
- 2 tablespoons cornflour + 3 tablespoons water (blended)

HHHHHHHHHHHHHHHHHHHHHHHHHHHHHHHHHHHH

Instructions:

1. In a wok, heat the groundnut oil. When sufficiently hot, add the spare ribs, deep frying until browned and crisp. As you will need to do this in batches, drain each fried batch using kitchen paper towel.

2. In a suitable pan, combine the chicken stock, sugar, chili bean sauce, rice wine, light soy sauce, dark soy sauce, garlic, spring onions, hoisin sauce, yellow bean sauce, and the cornflour blended with the water, bring to boil.

3. Add the fried ribs to the pan, cover with a lid and simmer for 60 minutes, until tender. Drain away the sauce while removing any of the remaining fat.

4. Heat the main oven to 360 degrees F.

5. Arrange the ribs on a baking rack set in a roasting pan and bake for between 15-18 minutes or until browned, remembering to baste every 4-5 minutes.

6. Take a meat cleaver and chop the ribs into pieces of approximately 2½" in length.

7. Place the ribs on a dinner platter and serve.

Recipe 7: Sweet Corn Soup with Crabmeat

You can find this soup in American, Chinese and Canadian cuisine. Made with crabmeat and creamed corn, it's a tasty and comforting fusion of flavors.

Makes: 4

Preparation Time: 30mins

Cook Time: 15mins

Total Cook Time: 45mins

Ingredient List:

- ¾ teaspoons ginger (finely chopped)
- ¾ cup canned crabmeat (drained)
- 2 teaspoons cornstarch
- 4 teaspoons water
- 3 cups chicken broth
- 1 (12 ounce) can corn (drained)
- 1 (14 ounce) can creamed corn
- 1 teaspoon light soy sauce
- ½ teaspoons sugar
- Dash black pepper (to taste)
- ½ teaspoons sesame oil
- 1 -2 green onions (finely chopped)

HHHHHHHHHHHHHHHHHHHHHHHHHHHHHHHHHHHHH

Instructions:

1. In a mixing bowl, add the ginger to the crabmeat and stir to combine.

2. In a second bowl, add the cornstarch and blend with the water.

3. In a saucepan, bring the broth, corn, creamed corn, soy sauce, sugar and black pepper to a boil, while occasionally stirring.

4. Add the crabmeat mixture and bring back to boil.

5. Give the cornstarch and water mixture a stir and add it to the soup, quickly stirring until thickened.

6. Take the soup off the heat.

7. Stir in the sesame oil and ladle it into bowls, sprinkled with finely chopped green onions.

Recipe 8: Crispy Asian Chicken Wings

Wings are an all-time favorite Chinese appetizer and make a super sharing dish for any occasion.

Makes: 12

Preparation Time: 20mins

Cook Time: 1hour 10mins

Total Cook Time: 9hours 30mins

Ingredient List:

- 2 pounds chicken wings
- 2 cloves garlic (peeled, smashed)
- 1½" piece ginger (peeled, coarsely chopped)
- Zest and juice of 1 fresh lime
- 2 tablespoons light brown sugar
- 2 tablespoons chili garlic sauce
- 2 tablespoons unseasoned rice vinegar
- 2 tablespoons soy sauce
- 3 tablespoons hoisin sauce
- 1½ teaspoons kosher salt
- 3 tablespoons sesame oil
- Sesame seeds (to garnish)
- Scallions (thinly sliced, to serve)
- Lime wedges (to garnish)

HHHHHHHHHHHHHHHHHHHHHHHHHHHHHHHHHHHHH

Instructions:

1. First prepare the chicken wings, by removing the tips and separating into drumettes and wings.

2. In a large bowl, whisk the garlic, ginger, lime zest, lime juice, brown sugar, garlic sauce, rice vinegar, soy sauce, hoisin sauce, kosher salt, and the sesame oil.

3. Place the chicken wings in a Ziploc bag and add the marinade. Seal the bag and turn the bag 6-7 times to evenly coat the chicken. Transfer to the fridge to chill overnight.

4. The next day, preheat the main oven to 350 degrees F.

5. Arrange the chicken wings, in a single layer on an aluminum foil lined cookie sheet, put the marinade to one side.

6. Bake in the oven for 60 minutes, or until browned and sufficiently cooked through. Flip the wings a few times to prevent them sticking.

7. Using a fine-mesh sieve, strain the marinade into a pan over moderate to high heat.

8. Pour in ½ cup of water and bring to boil, boil for 10 minutes. Add additional water if necessary to thin the liquid a little.

9. Scatter sesame seeds over the cooked wings, sprinkle with scallions and serve with lime wedges.

Recipe 9: Spinach and Edamame Egg Drop Soup

A traditional, bright soup for Chinese New Year.

Makes: 4

Preparation Time: 12mins

Cook Time: 8mins

Total Cook Time: 20mins

Ingredient List:

- 6 cups chicken stock
- 1½ teaspoons kosher salt (divided)
- 1 tablespoon ginger (finely grated)
- 1½ teaspoons cornstarch
- 1 tablespoon soy sauce
- 1 tablespoon toasted sesame oil
- 3 medium eggs
- 2 cups baby spinach
- 1½ cups edamame (cooked, shelled)
- 4 scallions (thinly sliced)

HHHHHHHHHHHHHHHHHHHHHHHHHHHHHHHHHHHH

Instructions:

1. In a large pan, bring the chicken stock, 1 teaspoon of salt and ginger to boil.

2. Add the cornstarch and soy sauce to a mixing bowl, and stir until silky.

3. Whisk the cornstarch-soy sauce mixture into the stock and cook for 1-2 minutes, until just thickened. Take off the heat.

4. In a second bowl, whisk the remaining ½ teaspoons of salt with the sesame oil, and eggs.

5. Gently whisk the broth and slowly and carefully add the egg mixture, making sure to scatter the eggs as they are cooking.

6. Add the spinach and edamame and stir, cook for 60 seconds until the spinach wilts.

7. Season the soup with salt and ladle into 4 soup bowls.

8. Garnish with thinly sliced scallions.

Recipe 10: Shrimp Toast

No Chinese banquet is complete without shrimp toast. Serve alongside a sweet and sour dipping sauce.

Makes: 4

Preparation Time: 10mins

Cook Time: 5mins

Total Cook Time: 15mins

Ingredient List:

- 4 slices white bread
- 8 ounces cooked peeled shrimp
- 1 teaspoon sesame oil
- 1 tablespoon soy sauce
- 2 garlic cloves (peeled, crushed)
- 1 large egg
- 1 tablespoon sesame seeds (toasted)
- Oil (for frying)

HHHHHHHHHHHHHHHHHHHHHHHHHHHHHHHHHHHHHHHH

Instructions:

1. First, remove the crusts from the bread.

2. Add the shrimp, sesame oil, soy sauce, garlic and egg to a food processor and blend until a paste-like consistency.

3. Evenly spread the smooth paste on top of the bread.

4. Sprinkle with sesame seeds, pressing the seeds into the bread.

5. Cut the slices of bread into small triangles.

6. In a wok, heat the oil and fry the shrimp toasts, sesame side facing upwards, until golden brown, this will take between 3-5 minutes. Watch carefully as you do not want them to burn.

7. Drain thoroughly before serving.

Chapter II – Main Dish Recipes

HHHHHHHHHHHHHHHHHHHHHHHHHHHHHHHHHHHHHHH

Recipe 11: Drunken Manila Clams

A quick and simple dish, with fresh Manila clams in Chinese Shaoxing wine for a delicious and light main course.

Makes: 2-3

Preparation Time: 10mins

Cook Time: 20mins

Total Cook Time: 30mins

Ingredient List:

- Sesame oil
- 1 (2") chunk fresh ginger (peeled, julienned)
- 1 pound fresh Manila clams
- 1½ cups Chinese Shaoxing wine
- 2 scallion stalks (julienned)
- Sea salt and white pepper

HHHHHHHHHHHHHHHHHHHHHHHHHHHHHHHHHHHHHHH

Instructions:

1. Heat a splash of sesame oil in a wok. Add the ginger and sauté for a couple of minutes until browned.

2. Toss in the clams and pour in the wine. Cover with a lid, cook for a few minutes then uncover and add the scallions. Season with salt and white pepper, stir quickly.

3. Discard any clams that have not opened, then serve the cooked clams in bowls.

Recipe 12: Vegetable Lo Mein

These yummy, fresh noodles are a marriage of tangy, sweet, sour, and, spicy flavors.

Makes: 3

Preparation Time: 10mins

Cook Time: 10mins

Total Cook Time: 20mins

Ingredient List:

- 1 tablespoon sweet soy sauce
- 1 tablespoon black bean sauce
- 1 tablespoon oyster sauce
- 1½ teaspoons cornstarch
- 2 teaspoons soy sauce
- 1½ teaspoons yuzu kosho seasoning
- 1 tablespoon Shaoxing wine
- 1 teaspoon fresh ginger (peeled, minced)
- 1½ teaspoons rice vinegar
- ¼ teaspoons caraway seeds (ground)
- 2 tablespoons canola oil
- 1 small bok choy (chopped)
- 4 ounces cabbage (shredded)
- 8 ounces lo mein noodles (cooked)
- 1 tablespoon dill (minced)
- 2 ounces pickled mustard greens (chopped)

HHHHHHHHHHHHHHHHHHHHHHHHHHHHHHHHHHHHHHH

Instructions:

1. Whisk together the sweet soy sauce, black bean sauce, oyster sauce, cornstarch, soy sauce, yuzu kosho seasoning, wine, ginger, rice vinegar, and ground caraway in a small bowl, set to one side.

2. Add the canola oil to a wok over high heat and add the bok choy and cabbage. Sauté for 5 minutes then add the noodles. After 60 seconds pour in the sauce along with the dill and mustard green. Cook for 2 minutes before spooning into bowls and serving.

Recipe 13: Moo Goo Gai Pan

Next time you have a craving for something hot and sour, skip the takeout and get cooking!

Makes: 2

Preparation Time: 10mins

Cook Time: 20mins

Total Cook Time: 1hour

Ingredient List:

Marinade:

- 1 tablespoon rice vinegar
- 1 tablespoon soy sauce
- 1 teaspoon cornstarch
- ½ pound skinless, boneless chicken breast (chopped)

Moo Goo Gai Pan:

- 1 tablespoon peanut oil
- 2 garlic cloves (peeled, minced)
- 1½ cups snow peas
- 1½ cups button mushrooms (sliced)
- ¼ cup water chestnuts (sliced)
- ½ cup bamboo shoots

Sauce:

- ½ cup chicken broth
- 1 tablespoon rice vinegar
- 1 tablespoon soy sauce
- ½ teaspoons sesame oil
- ½ teaspoons granulated sugar
- 1 tablespoon cornstarch dissolved in 2 tablespoons water

- White pepper

HHHHHHHHHHHHHHHHHHHHHHHHHHHHHHHHHHHHHHH

Instructions:

1. Whisk the marinade ingredients (vinegar, soy sauce, and cornstarch) together in a bowl. Add the chicken and set aside for half an hour.

2. Over moderately high heat, add the peanut oil to a skillet and sauté the chicken for several minutes. Transfer to a plate.

3. Add the garlic, snow peas, and mushrooms to the skillet. Cook for 5 minutes.

4. Add the water chestnuts, bamboo shoots, and browned chicken to the skillet, sauté for 2 minutes.

5. Add the sauce ingredients (chicken broth, vinegar, soy sauce, sesame oil, sugar, cornstarch, white pepper) and cook while stirring until the sauce begins to thicken.

6. Take off the heat and serve.

Recipe 14: Beef and Broccoli Stir-Fry

A classic and well-loved dish, it is easy to see why this saucy beef and fresh broccoli stir-fry is such a firm-favorite.

Makes: 4

Preparation Time: 10mins

Cook Time: 10mins

Total Cook Time: 20mins

Ingredient List:

- ¾ pound flank steak (cut into ¼" thick slices)
- 1½ teaspoons cornstarch
- 2 teaspoons + 1 tablespoon Shaoxing wine
- 1 teaspoon sesame oil
- Salt and black pepper
- ½" chunk fresh ginger (peeled, minced)
- 2 tablespoons chicken stock
- 2 tablespoons soy sauce
- 2 tablespoons oyster sauce
- 2 tablespoons peanut oil
- 1 garlic clove (peeled, minced)
- 1 yellow onion (peeled, sliced thinly)
- 1 tablespoon black fermented beans (mashed)
- 12 ounces broccoli (cut into florets)
- White rice (cooked, for serving)

HHHHHHHHHHHHHHHHHHHHHHHHHHHHHHHHHHHHHHH

Instructions:

1. Add the beef, cornstarch, 2 teaspoons rice wine, sesame oil, salt, pepper, and ginger to a bowl. Toss to combine.

2. In a second bowl, whisk together the chicken stock, soy sauce, oyster sauce, and remaining rice wine.

3. Heat half of the peanut oil in a skillet over high heat; add the garlic, onions, and black beans, sauté for 30-45 seconds. Arrange the marinated beef in the pan in a single layer cook for 60 seconds without stirring. Take the beef out of the skillet and set on a plate.

4. Heat the remaining oil in the skillet, sauté the onion in it for 2 minutes before adding the broccoli and cooking for another 2 minutes.

5. Pop the beef back in the skillet along with any juices that have collected on the plate. Stir well and cook for a couple more minutes before dishing out and serving with rice.

Recipe 15: Sweet 'n Sour Oyster Pork Meatballs

Succulent and juicy Sichuan-style meatballs are sautéed until crispy, then cooked in a sticky sweet 'n sour sauce.

Makes: 2-3

Preparation Time: 15mins

Cook Time: 20mins

Total Cook Time: 35mins

Ingredient List:

- 3 cups canola oil
- 10 fresh oysters (shucked, finely chopped)
- 10 ounces ground pork
- 6 garlic cloves (minced)
- 2 scallions (minced)
- White of 1 medium egg
- 1½" chunk fresh ginger (peeled, minced)
- ¼ cup cornstarch
- 2 tablespoons soy sauce
- ¼ cup red chili bean paste
- 2 tablespoons granulated sugar
- 2 tablespoons dry sherry
- 1 tablespoon black vinegar
- Steamed white rice (for serving)

HHHHHHHHHHHHHHHHHHHHHHHHHHHHHHHHHHHHH

Instructions:

1. Pour the canola oil into a wok with a flat bottom and heat until it registers 350 degrees F.

2. In a large bowl, add the oysters, pork, half of the garlic, scallions, egg white, and ginger. Use hands to mix until combined. Rolls the mixture into 1½" meatballs. Roll each bowl in cornstarch.

3. Cook the meatballs in the canola oil in two batches, cooking each batch for 5 minutes, while stirring. Take out of the wok using a slotted spoon and set to one side to rest on kitchen paper.

4. Drain away all but 3 tablespoons of the cooking oil and over moderately high heat, stir in the remaining garlic, cook for 3-4 minutes until fragrant before adding the soy sauce, chili bean paste, sugar, sherry, and vinegar. Bring to a boil for several minutes until the sauce is sticky and thick.

5. Return the meatballs to the wok and cook for a few minutes until hot through.

6. Serve with steamed rice.

Recipe 16: Black Chinese Mushroom Chicken

Chinese mushrooms have a powerfully rich and earthy flavor which bring depth to this yummy chicken dish.

Makes: 2-3

Preparation Time: 10mins

Cook Time: 15mins

Total Cook Time: 25mins

Ingredient List:

- 2 tablespoons canola oil
- 2" chunk ginger (peeled, grated)
- 2 garlic cloves (peeled, chopped)
- 2 large breast chicken (pounded, sliced into strips)
- 14 dried Chinese black mushrooms (soaked in warm water for 25 minutes, drained)
- 3 tablespoons oyster sauce
- 3 tablespoons soy sauce
- 2 teaspoons Shaoxing wine
- ¼ cup chicken broth
- 1 tablespoon cornstarch dissolved in 3 tablespoons water
- 1 scallion (sliced)

HHHHHHHHHHHHHHHHHHHHHHHHHHHHHHHHHHHHHH

Instructions:

1. Over moderately high heat, place a wok. Add the canola oil and then add the ginger and garlic, stir-fry for 30-40 seconds.

2. Add the sliced chicken and fry for 60 seconds.

3. Add the mushrooms, cook for a few minutes before pouring in the oyster sauce, soy sauce, wine, broth, and cornstarch. Stir while cooking for another few minutes.

4. Stir in the sliced scallions and serve straight away.

Recipe 17: Spicy Eggplant with Garlic

Eggplant is steamed then stir-fried in a spicy garlic sauce, to make a super yummy vegetarian main that is delicious served with fluffy white rice.

Makes: 4

Preparation Time: 15mins

Cook Time: 20mins

Total Cook Time: 35mins

Ingredient List:

- 1 teaspoon red chili flakes (crushed)
- ¼ cup soy sauce
- 2 tablespoons black vinegar
- 1 teaspoon fine salt
- 1 tablespoon granulated sugar
- 4 medium eggplants (each cut into 2" thick slices, then sliced into 6 wedges)
- 2 tablespoons canola oil
- 10 garlic cloves (minced)
- 3" chunk fresh ginger (minced)
- 1 teaspoon sesame oil
- ¼ cup scallions (minced)
- Steamed white rice

HHHHHHHHHHHHHHHHHHHHHHHHHHHHHHHHHHHHH

Instructions:

1. In a small bowl, whisk together the crushed chili flakes, soy sauce, black vinegar, salt, and sugar. Set to one side.

2. Arrange half of the chopped eggplant in a pie dish.

3. Fit a wok with a bamboo steamer base, pour in water to reach ¾" of the way up and bring to a boil. Place the pie dish in the base of the steamer. Cover with the steamer lid.

4. Steam the eggplant for several minutes until fork-tender.

5. Cook the remaining eggplant in exactly the same way.

6. Take a second wok and set over high heat.

7. Add the oil, when it is very hot, add the minced garlic and ginger, stir-fry for 15 seconds. Add the steamed eggplant, fry for 25 seconds.

8. Pour in the sauce set-aside earlier, stir well. Stir-fry for 3-4 minutes until it thickens.

9. Take the wok off the heat, spoon onto a serving platter, drizzle with sesame oil and scatter over minced scallions.

10. Serve with steamed white rice.

Recipe 18: Buddha's Delight

Buddha's Delight, or Lo Han Jai, is a vegetarian dish packed full with Chinese delights such as Chinese black mushrooms, wood ears, and mung bean noodles. It's the perfect recipe to welcome in Chinese New Year.

Makes: 6

Preparation Time: 15mins

Cook Time: 15mins

Total Cook Time: 30mins

Ingredient List:

- 2 tablespoons canola oil
- 3 slivers ginger
- 3 tablespoons fermented red bean curd
- 3 garlic cloves (peeled, sliced)
- 1 leek (chopped)
- 5 dried Chinese black mushrooms (rehydrated)
- ¼ cup dried wood ears (rehydrated)
- 2 tablespoons Shaoxing rice wine
- 3 cups Napa cabbage (chopped)
- 2 sticks dried bean threads (rehydrated, chopped)
- 2 tablespoons soy sauce
- 1 teaspoon sesame oil
- 1 cup vegetable broth
- 2 teaspoons granulated sugar
- 1 bundle mung bean noodles (soaked, drained, chopped)

HHHHHHHHHHHHHHHHHHHHHHHHHHHHHHHHHHHHHH

Instructions:

1. Over moderately high heat, add the canola oil and ginger to a wok.

2. Sauté the ginger for 30-4 seconds then add the bean curd. Use a wooden spoon to break up the curd.

3. Add the garlic, leeks, rehydrated black mushrooms, and rehydrated wood ears. Stir-fry for 60 seconds.

4. Pour in the wine and cook for 60 seconds more.

5. Add the cabbage, bean threads and turn the heat to the highest possible setting. After two minutes add the soy sauce, sesame oil, vegetable broth, and sugar. Stir well, cover and turn the heat down a little lower. Cook for 5-6 minutes then uncover, crank the heat back up, add the noodles and stir until the majority of the liquid has evaporated.

6. Ladle into bowls and serve.

Recipe 19: Shrimp with Lobster Sauce and Vegetables

A delicious fish dish to bring health and prosperity to your New Year celebrations. Don't be fooled by the name though, authentic Chinese shrimp with lobster sauce actually contains no lobster!

Makes: 3-4

Preparation Time: 10mins

Cook Time: 15mins

Total Cook Time: 25mins

Ingredient List:

- 12 ounces fresh shrimp (peeled, veined)
- Pinch each sugar and salt
- 2 tablespoons canola oil
- 2 garlic cloves (peeled, sliced thinly)
- 1" chunk ginger (peeled, sliced thinly)
- 1 cup chicken stock
- ½ tablespoons Shaoxing wine
- ¾ cup mixed frozen vegetables
- ½ teaspoons soy sauce
- 3 pinches white pepper
- 1 tablespoon cornstarch dissolved in 2 tablespoons water
- White of 1 medium egg (beaten)

HHHHHHHHHHHHHHHHHHHHHHHHHHHHHHHHHHHH

Instructions:

1. Season the shrimp with sugar and salt.

2. Heat the canola oil in a wok over moderate heat. Add the garlic and ginger, sauté for 2 minutes. Add the seasoned shrimp to the wok. Fry until the shrimp is half cooked before pouring in the chicken stock and wine. Bring to a boil.

3. Add the frozen veggies, soy sauce and a pinch more salt, sugar, and white pepper.

4. Bring the mixture to a simmer and while stirring, add in the cornstarch mixture.

5. Bring back to the boil.

6. Drizzle the beaten egg onto the surface of the mixture, swirl three times using a chopstick. As soon as the egg forms silky threads take off the heat.

7. Serve.

Recipe 20: Char Siu Barbecue Pork Belly

Succulent pork belly slow-cooked in a Chinese barbecue marinade is the ultimate comfort food.

Makes: 4-6

Preparation Time: 15mins

Cook Time: 45mins

Total Cook Time: 3hours 30mins

Ingredient List:

- 1 pound pork belly (skin removed)
- 2 tablespoons soy sauce
- 2 tablespoons Shaoxing wine
- 2 tablespoons granulated sugar
- ½ tablespoons hoisin sauce
- 2 garlic cloves (peeled, minced)
- ½ teaspoons Chinese 5-spice seasoning
- 2 tablespoons honey

HHHHHHHHHHHHHHHHHHHHHHHHHHHHHHHHHHHHH

Instructions:

1. Place the pork belly in a large dish.

2. Whisk together the soy sauce, wine, sugar, hoisin, garlic, and 5-spice. Pour over the pork. Rub the marinade into the pork and chill for 2½ hours.

3. Preheat the main oven to 325 degrees F.

4. Transfer the pork to a roasting tin. Brush the top and sides of the pork with honey. Place in the oven and roast for 45 minutes, flipping halfway and basting with honey.

5. When the outsides have begun to blacken, and the center feels firm, take the pork out of the oven, and allow to rest for 10-12 minutes.

6. Slice thinly and serve.

Recipe 21: Shanghai-Style Beef and Tomato Stir Fry

This lesser-known Chinese dish is very popular in Shanghai and is a delicious combination of tender flanks steak and rich Chinese tomato sauce.

Makes: 2

Preparation Time: 10mins

Cook Time: 10mins

Total Cook Time: 45mins

Ingredient List:

- 8 ounces trimmed flank steak (thinly sliced across the grain)
- 2 teaspoons garlic (peeled, minced)
- 1 teaspoon ginger (peeled, minced)
- 2 tablespoons soy sauce
- 1 teaspoon Chinese Shaoxing cooking wine
- 1 teaspoon cornstarch
- 2 teaspoons canola oil
- 8 ounces fresh plum tomatoes (cored, chopped)
- 2 teaspoons granulated sugar
- ¼ cup basil leaves
- White rice (cooked, for serving)

HHHHHHHHHHHHHHHHHHHHHHHHHHHHHHHHHHHHH

Instructions:

1. Add the sliced beef, garlic, ginger, soy sauce, wine, and cornstarch to a large bowl. Stir and allow to marinate for 20-25 minutes.

2. Heat a splash of canola oil in a skillet with high sides; add the tomatoes and sauté for 3-4 minutes. Add the sugar and marinated beef, cook for 2-3 minutes, stirring often.

3. Take off the heat, scatter with basil leaves and serve with white rice.

Recipe 22: Fresh Crab Claws in Sweet and Sour Sauce

The beauty of Asian cuisine is the delicate balance of sweet and sour flavors to create a harmonious dish.

Makes: 2

Preparation Time: 10mins

Cook Time: 15mins

Total Cook Time: 25mins

Ingredient List:

- 1½ tablespoons canola oil
- 3-4 slices fresh ginger (minced)
- 1 clove garlic (minced)
- 8 ounces fresh crab claws (rinsed, patted dry)
- 1 tablespoon chili sauce
- 1 tablespoon tomato ketchup
- ½ teaspoons granulated sugar
- ½ teaspoons oyster sauce
- ½ teaspoons cornstarch mixed in ½ cup water
- ½ egg (beaten)
- Small handful fresh cilantro (chopped)

HHHHHHHHHHHHHHHHHHHHHHHHHHHHHHHHHHHHH

Instructions:

1. Add the oil to a wok and place over moderately high heat. When the oil is hot, add the ginger and garlic, sauté for 3-4 minutes then add the crab claws. Stir 3-4 times before adding the chili sauce, ketchup, sugar, and oyster sauce. Toss to coat the crab in the sauce. Add the cornstarch mixture and stir well until incorporated.

2. Bring to a boil and then immediately drop in the beaten egg. Cook for 1-2 minutes until the egg has set. Gently stir to distribute the egg into the sauce.

3. Spoon into serving bowls and scatter with fresh cilantro.

Recipe 23: Scallion and Ginger Basa fish

Basa is a member of the catfish family; therefore, it's white and meaty, making it a perfect fish for cooking in zingy Chinese sauces.

Makes: 2-3

Preparation Time: 10mins

Cook Time: 20mins

Total Cook Time: 40mins

Ingredient List:

- 1 (10 ounce) boneless Basa fish fillet (chopped)
- 1 teaspoon cornstarch mixed with 1 teaspoon Shaoxing wine
- 1½ tablespoons canola oil
- 2" chunk fresh ginger (peeled, thinly sliced)
- ½ tablespoons oyster sauce
- ½ tablespoons soy sauce
- ½ teaspoons cornstarch
- 1 teaspoon granulated sugar
- ¼ teaspoons sesame oil
- 3½ tablespoons water
- Salt and white pepper
- 2 scallions (chopped)

HHHHHHHHHHHHHHHHHHHHHHHHHHHHHHHHHHHHH

Instructions:

1. Add the chopped fish to a bowl, pour over the cornstarch mixture and gently toss to combine. Set aside for 10-12 minutes.

2. Add the canola oil to a wok over moderate heat, when hot, add the ginger and fish. Cook while stirring until the fish is half-cooked.

3. Whisk together the oyster sauce, soy sauce, cornstarch, sugar, sesame oil, water, and a pinch each of salt and white pepper in a small bowl. Pour over the fish in the wok.

4. Cook until the fish is white throughout.

5. Scatter with scallions, stir a final few times and transfer to a serving bowl.

Recipe 24: Honey and Walnut Shrimp

This game-changing seafood dish with a sweet honey and walnut sauce is guaranteed to please the whole family.

Makes: 4-6

Preparation Time: 10mins

Cook Time: 10mins

Total Cook Time: 20mins

Ingredient List:

Sauce:

- ⅔ cup full-fat mayo
- 1 teaspoon red chili flakes (crushed)
- 1 teaspoon powdered garlic
- 4 tablespoons honey
- ½ teaspoons salt
- 1 tablespoon sweetened condensed milk

Shrimp:

- 1 cup water
- ⅔ cup granulated sugar
- ½ cup walnuts (halved)
- 2 pounds fresh shrimp (peeled, tailed, veined)
- 1 cup flour
- 3 medium eggs beaten with 2 tablespoons water
- 1 cup panko breadcrumbs
- 4 tablespoons canola oil

HHHHHHHHHHHHHHHHHHHHHHHHHHHHHHHHHHHHHHHH

Instructions:

1. Whisk the sauce ingredients together in a bowl (the mayo, chili flakes, garlic, honey, salt, and milk). Set to one side.

2. In a small saucepan add the water and sugar, bring to a boil. Add the walnuts and boil for 2 minutes more. Drain the liquid from the pan and set the walnuts aside on a plate to cool.

3. To a large ziplock bag, add the shrimp and flour. Seal and shake to coat the shrimp.

4. In a small bowl, add the beaten egg/water.

5. Add the panko breadcrumbs to a second bowl.

6. Dip each shrimp first in the beaten egg and then in the breadcrumbs.

7. Heat the canola oil in a skillet over moderate heat, add the coated shrimp and fry for 5-6 minutes until browned.

8. Toss the coated shrimp in the set aside honey/milk sauce.

9. Serve straight away scattered with walnuts.

Recipe 25: Roasted Cashew Chicken

Tender marinated chicken and crunchy roasted cashews make for a deliciously textured dish.

Makes: 4

Preparation Time: 10mins

Cook Time: 20mins

Total Cook Time: 30mins

Ingredient List:

- 1½ pounds skinless, boneless chicken (chopped into 1" chunks)
- ½ teaspoons sea salt
- ¼ teaspoons black pepper
- 1 tablespoon cornstarch
- 2 tablespoons canola oil
- ½ cup yellow onion (peeled, diced)
- 8 ounces canned water chestnuts (sliced)
- 4 garlic cloves (peeled, grated)
- 2 tablespoons rice wine vinegar
- ⅓ cup water
- 5 tablespoons hoisin sauce
- ¾ cup roasted cashew
- Cooked rice (for serving)
- Scallions (chopped, for garnish)

HHHHHHHHHHHHHHHHHHHHHHHHHHHHHHHHHHH

Instructions:

1. Add the chicken pieces, salt, pepper, and cornstarch to a food storage container, seal and shake to coat the chicken.

2. Heat the oil in a skillet over moderately high heat, add the coated chicken and onion, Sauté for 10 minutes, while stirring.

3. Toss in the water chestnuts and garlic, sauté for 3-4 minutes, then add the rice wine vinegar, water, and hoisin. Cook for a final 3-4 minutes, checking that the chicken is cooked.

4. Take off the heat and stir in the roasted cashews.

5. Spoon into bowls, along with rice and garnish with chopped scallions.

Recipe 26: Long Life Noodles

No New Year's food spread would be complete without a plate of steaming hot long life noodles, or yi mein, which are thought to bring good luck for a long, happy, and healthy life.

Makes: 4

Preparation Time: 15mins

Cook Time: 45mins

Total Cook Time: 50mins

Ingredient List:

- 8 ounces chicken with bones (chopped into pieces)
- 14 ounces fresh egg noodles
- 2 ounces fresh snow peas
- 2 tablespoons canola oil
- 1 clove garlic (peeled, minced)
- 1 teaspoon ginger (peeled, minced)
- 2 ounces shiitake mushrooms (sliced thinly)
- 2 ounces carrots (peeled, julienned)
- 2 ounces bell pepper (diced)
- 4 tablespoons oyster sauce
- 1 teaspoon salt
- 1 cup chicken broth
- 3 tablespoons cornstarch dissolved in 2 tablespoons water
- 2 scallions (chopped)

HHHHHHHHHHHHHHHHHHHHHHHHHHHHHHHHHHHHHHH

Instructions:

1. Bring a pot of water to a boil and toss in the pieces of chicken. Cook for just under half an hour. Take out of the pot and set to one side to cool a little.

2. Remove all bones and flesh from the chicken and shred the meat using a fork.

3. Bring a second pot of water over high heat to a boil. Add the egg noodles and cook for 3 minutes, until al dente. Drain and set to one side.

4. Blanch the peas in boiling water and then immediately plunge into ice water. Drain and set to one side.

5. In a wok over moderately high heat add the canola oil, sauté the garlic and ginger for 30-40 seconds, then add the mushrooms and carrots. Cook for 3 minutes before adding the pepper and shredded chicken. Cook for a minute then add the oyster sauce, salt, and chicken broth. Bring to a boil and stir in the cornstarch.

6. When the sauce becomes thicker add the peas, scallions, and noodles to the wok. Cook for 2½ minutes then transfer to serving bowls.

Recipe 27: Old Beijing-Style Noodles

This fresh and vibrant noodle bowl is many Beijinger's dish of choice when they want something quick, delicious, and satisfying.

Makes: 3-4

Preparation Time: 10mins

Cook Time: 40mins

Total Cook Time: 50mins

Ingredient List:

- 4 ounces soybean paste
- 2 ounces hoisin sauce
- 1 tablespoon canola oil
- 1 pound pork belly (chopped finely)
- 1 tablespoon Shaoxing wine
- 1" chunk ginger (peeled, grated)
- 1 teaspoon granulated sugar
- 10 ounces fresh wheat noodles

Topping:

- 2 ounces cucumber (julienned)
- 2 ounces scallions (sliced)
- 2 ounces radish (julienned)

HHHHHHHHHHHHHHHHHHHHHHHHHHHHHHHHHHH

Instructions:

1. Whisk together the soybean paste and hoisin sauce in a small bowl, set to one side.

2. Heat the canola oil in a wok over moderately low heat, add the finely chopped pork belly and sauté for 4-5 minutes.

3. Transfer the pork to a side plate.

4. Use the pork fat in the wok to cook the set-aside hoisin sauce/paste for 60 seconds.

5. Add the wine, ginger, sugar, and cooked pork, cook for 30 seconds. Stir well and pour in a cup of water. Bring to a boil, then turn down to a simmer and cook for 30 minutes.

6. In the meantime, cook the noodles according to packet directions. Drain the noodles and divide between 3-4 bowls.

7. Top with the cooked pork mixture and garnish with the fresh cucumber, scallions, and radish.

Recipe 28: Mapo Tofu

Mapo Tofu is a fiery hot dish of tofu and ground beef in a spicy Sichuan peppercorn sauce. Grab an ice-cold Chinese beer; it's gonna get hot!

Makes: 4

Preparation Time: 10mins

Cook Time: 15mins

Total Cook Time: 25mins

Ingredient List:

- ½ cup Sichuan red chilli oil (hong you)
- 6" chunk fresh ginger (peeled, minced)
- 6 garlic cloves (peeled, minced)
- 6 ounces ground beef
- 1 red chili (seeded, minced)
- 4 scallions (thinly sliced)
- 2½ tablespoons red chili bean paste
- 1 tablespoon black fermented soybeans
- 1¼ cups chicken broth
- 14 ounces firm tofu (drained, chopped into 1" cubes)*
- 1 tablespoon soy sauce
- 1 tablespoon granulated sugar
- ¼ cup cornstarch dissolved in 6 tablespoons water
- Salt
- ¼ teaspoons Sichuan pepper (ground)
- Steamed white rice

HHHHHHHHHHHHHHHHHHHHHHHHHHHHHHHHHHHHHH

Instructions:

1. In a wok with a flat bottom, heat the chili oil over moderately high heat.

2. Add the ginger and garlic, cook for 60 seconds, Add the ground beef, sauté for 5 minutes stirring with a wooden spoon to break up the meat.

3. Add the chili, scallions, bean paste, and soybeans, sauté for 2 minutes.

4. Pour in the broth and add the tofu, bring to a boil while stirring very carefully.

5. Add the soy sauce and sugar, cook for 60 seconds until the sugar has dissolved.

6. While stirring, pour in the cornstarch mixture a little at a time. Cook for 2 minutes, until the sauce, has become thick.

7. Season with salt. Transfer to a serving dish, sprinkle with Sichuan pepper and serve on top of white rice.

*Place the tofu in a large bowl, cover with 3 cups of salted boiling water and set aside for 15 minutes. Drain and pat dry with kitchen paper towels.

Recipe 29: New Year Red Hot Pot

This hearty hot chicken soup is a New Year's staple as its vibrant red color is thought to bring prosperity and good fortune for the year ahead. It is generally served in a large pot placed straight on the table with a number of raw accompaniments that guests cook for themselves in the broth.

Makes: 6-8

Preparation Time: 15mins

Cook Time: 3hours

Total Cook Time: 3hours 15mins

Ingredient List:

- 3 pounds leftover pork bones
- 1 whole (3½ pound) chicken
- 8 cups water
- 2 scallions (sliced in half)
- 2" chunk ginger (peeled, smashed)
- 6 dried whole chilies
- ⅓ cup Chinese chili garlic sauce
- 2 ounces bean thread noodles
- 1 pound beef (sliced thinly)
- 14 ounces firm tofu
- 2 pounds Napa cabbage and bok choy
- Mixed cooked seafood (scallops, prawns, calamari, etc.)

HHHHHHHHHHHHHHHHHHHHHHHHHHHHHHHHHHHH

Instructions:

1. In a large pot add the pork bones and chicken. Pour over enough water to cover by an extra inch.

2. Bring to a boil for 5-6 minutes.

3. Drain away the liquid. Rinse clean the pork bones and chicken.

4. Return the pork bones and chicken to the pot along with 8 cups fresh water. Bring to a boil then turn down to a simmer. Skim away any foam off the surface. Cover and cook for 2 hours.

5. Strain the broth and set to one side. Discard the chicken and bones or use in another recipe.

6. Over high heat, return the strained broth to the pan along with the scallions, ginger, and chilies. Simmer for half an hour, discard the scallions, chilies and ginger chunk. Stir in the chili garlic sauce.

7. Set the broth on the table and keep at a simmer/boil using a portable stove top.

8. Arrange the raw ingredients on plates around the broth pot.

9. Invite guests to dig in a cook their chosen accompaniments!

Recipe 30: Mongolian Crispy Beef

Thin slices of steak are cooked in a thick and sticky, sweet and salty sauce. Totally delicious!

Makes: 4

Preparation Time: 10mins

Cook Time: 15mins

Total Cook Time: 25mins

Ingredient List:

- 2 tablespoons sesame oil
- ½ cup water
- ⅓ cup soy sauce
- 2 teaspoons ginger (grated)
- ½ cup brown sugar
- 3 cloves garlic (peeled, pressed)
- 1 pound flank steak (thinly sliced)
- ¼ cup cornstarch
- ½ teaspoons kosher salt
- ½ teaspoons black pepper
- ½ cup canola oil
- 2 scallions (sliced)
- Sesame seeds

HHHHHHHHHHHHHHHHHHHHHHHHHHHHHHHHHHHHHH

Instructions:

1. Over moderate heat, add the sesame oil, water, soy sauce, ginger, sugar, and garlic to a saucepan. Cook for 7-8 minutes, until the liquid reduces. Take off the heat.

2. Add the sliced steak to a bowl and sprinkle with the cornstarch, kosher salt, and black pepper.

3. Heat the canola oil in a skillet and arrange the steak in a single layer in the skillet (cook in batches if necessary). Cook for 2 minutes each side over moderately high heat. Transfer the steak to a plate.

4. Add the set-aside sauce to the skillet along with the browned steak, cook for 3-4 minutes, over moderately low heat until nice and thick.

5. Scatter with scallions and sesame seeds, serve.

Chapter III – Sweet Recipes

HHHHHHHHHHHHHHHHHHHHHHHHHHHHHHHHHHHHHHHHH

Recipe 31: Pineapple Cakes

Chinese pineapple cakes, pronounced Feng Li Su, are often served around Chinese New Year.

Makes: 24

Preparation Time: 15mins

Cook Time: 25mins

Total Cook Time: 40mins

Ingredient List:

- 1 cup unsalted butter (at room temperature)
- ¼ cup powdered sugar
- 2 large eggs
- ½ teaspoon vanilla essence
- 2½ cups all-purpose flour
- ¼ cup cornstarch
- ¼ teaspoons salt
- 1 cup pineapple jam

HHHHHHHHHHHHHHHHHHHHHHHHHHHHHHHHHHHHHH

Instructions:

1. In the bowl of an electric food mixer, using a paddle attachment combine the butter with the powdered sugar. Cream on moderate speed for 6-8 minutes, until fluffy and light.

2. Add the 2 eggs and beat to incorporate. Add the vanilla essence and combine.

3. In a bowl, stir the flour into the cornstarch and salt and add to the mixer bowl, beating to combine fully. The dough needs to be pliable and soft.

4. Turn the dough out onto a sheet of plastic kitchen wrap, wrap and transfer to the fridge for half an hour, until firm.

5. Preheat the main oven to 325 degrees F. Line 5-6 cookie sheets with parchment.

6. Roll the dough into 1" balls and arrange in a single layer, and not touch on the cookie sheets.

7. Gently using the palm of your hand, flatten each of the balls and add 1 teaspoon of jam into the center.

8. Carefully, pinch the edges of the dough around the jam; this will help to seal it.

9. Bake in the oven for 20-25 minutes, until golden.

10. Allow to cool on a wire baking rack.

11. Serve.

Recipe 32: Almond Cookies

The secret to this recipe is the inclusion of lard rather than butter or margarine as it gives the cookies their authentic flavor. You can though if you prefer to, swap it for butter or margarine.

Makes: 48

Preparation Time: 40mins

Cook Time: 15mins

Total Cook Time: 55mins

Ingredient List:

- 2¾ cup all-purpose flour (sifted)
- 1 cup white sugar
- ½ teaspoons bicarb of soda
- ½ teaspoons salt
- 1 cup lard
- 1 medium egg
- 1 teaspoon almond essence
- 48 almonds

HHHHHHHHHHHHHHHHHHHHHHHHHHHHHHHHHHHH

Instructions:

1. Preheat the main oven to 325 degrees F.

2. In a mixing bowl, sift the flour, sugar, bicarb, and salt.

3. Cut in the lard to the dry ingredients until the mixture is the consistency of cornmeal.

4. Add the egg along with the almond essence and mix to combine.

5. Roll the dough into 1" balls and arrange them on an ungreased baking sheet, around 2" apart.

6. Pop an almond on top of each cookie, pressing down to flatten.

7. Bake in the oven for 15-20 minutes, until golden.

Recipe 33: Peanut Puffs

Addictive, moreish peanut treats are a popular Chinese New Year treat. Deep-fried to perfection your family is sure to want more!

Makes: 45

Preparation Time: 15mins

Cook Time: 15mins

Total Cook Time: 30mins

Ingredient List:

- Pastry Dough
- 3 cups cake flour (sifted)
- 3½ tablespoons unsalted butter (softened)
- 4 tablespoons peanut oil
- ¼ cup sugar
- 2 large eggs
- Oil (for frying)
- Peanut Filling:
- 1 ounce white sesame seeds
- ⅓ cup roasted peanuts
- ¼ cup sugar

HHHHHHHHHHHHHHHHHHHHHHHHHHHHHHHHHHHHHHH

Instructions:

1. In a bowl combine the flour, butter, peanut oil, sugar and eggs and mix to make a soft and smooth dough.

2. Over moderately low heat, heat a saucepan. Add the sesame seeds and toast until golden, taking care not to burn. Set to one side.

3. Using a food blender, grind the peanuts until you achieve a coarse texture.

4. Transfer the ground peanuts to a bowl and add the sesame seeds along with the sugar. Stir to combine.

5. Take a rolling pin and roll the pastry dough into a thin sheet.

6. Using a 1¾" cookie cutter, cut the pastry into rounds.

7. Place ½ teaspoons of the peanut filling into the middle of the round. Fold over, press and pinch to seal.

8. Heat a pan with the oil and in batches, deep-fry the peanut puffs, until golden.

9. Using a slotted spoon, remove the puffs from the oil and lay on a platter, lined with kitchen paper.

10. Allow to cool before transferring to a re-sealable, airtight container.

Recipe 34: Chinese Banana Fritters

Who doesn't lust after crispy, fried banana fritters?

Makes: 4

Preparation Time: 30mins

Cook Time: 25mins

Total Cook Time: 55mins

Ingredient List:

- 2 egg whites
- 3 tablespoons plain flour
- 3 tablespoons cornflour
- 4 tablespoons water
- ½ cup oil
- 5 ripe bananas (peeled, cut into bite-sized pieces)
- ½ cup confectioner's sugar

HHHHHHHHHHHHHHHHHHHHHHHHHHHHHHHHHHHHHH

Instructions:

1. In a bowl, whisk the egg whites until they begin to form soft peaks.

2. Add the flour, cornflour, and water to the egg whites to form a batter.

3. Heat the oil in a frying pan.

4. Dip the pieces of banana into the flour mixture and two or three at a time, carefully drop them into the hot oil.

5. Fry until golden, remove from the oil and drain on kitchen paper towel.

6. Dust with confectioner's sugar.

Recipe 35: New Year Cake

Nian Gao or New Year Cake has a history going back at least 1,000 years and so is perfect for your Chinese feast.

Makes: 10 (5 cakes)

Preparation Time: 10mins

Cook Time: 50mins

Total Cook Time: 1hour

Ingredient List:

- 1 pound Mochiko sweet rice flour
- ¾ cup vegetable oil
- 3 medium eggs
- 2½ cups milk
- ¾ cup sugar (to taste)
- 1 tablespoon baking soda
- 1 (14 ounce) can red azuki beans

HHHHHHHHHHHHHHHHHHHHHHHHHHHHHHHHHHHHHH

Instructions:

1. In the bowl of an electric food mixer, combine the rice flour, vegetable oil, eggs, milk, 1 cup sugar and baking soda. First, beat at moderate speed for 2 minutes, and then beat at high speed for another 2 minutes.

2. Sprinkle a little Mochiko flour over a 13x9" lightly-oiled casserole dish.

3. Spread half of the batter on the bottom of the casserole dish, spoon the beans on top and spread evenly.

4. Top the beans with the remaining batter.

5. Bake in the main oven for 40-50 minutes, at a temperature of 350 degrees F.

Recipe 36: Bananas with Cinnamon Coconut Sauce

When you think you can't possibly eat anymore and it's time for dessert, then this banana, cinnamon and coconut delight will change your mind!

Makes: 4

Preparation Time: 15mins

Cook Time: 15mins

Total Cook Time: 30

Ingredient List:

- 4 ripe bananas (peeled, cut into quarters)
- ½ cup coconut cream
- 1½ cups coconut milk
- ½ teaspoons cinnamon
- 2 tablespoons sugar
- 1 tablespoon cornstarch mixed in 3 tablespoons coconut milk
- Mint leaves (to garnish)

HHHHHHHHHHHHHHHHHHHHHHHHHHHHHHHHHHHH

Instructions:

1. First, steam the bananas in a steamer over a boiling water-filled wok.

2. In a pan, bring the coconut cream and milk to a boil. Add the cinnamon followed by the sugar and stir to combine.

3. Briefly stir the cornstarch and coconut milk and add to the pan, stirring to thicken.

4. Arrange the steamed banana in serving bowls and pour the cinnamon coconut sauce over the top.

5. Garnish with mint leaves.

Recipe 37: Fortune Cookies

Homemade fortune cookies are the very best way to celebrate Chinese New Year.

Makes: 10

Preparation Time: 15mins

Cook Time: 15mins

Total Cook Time: 30mins

Ingredient List:

- Whites of 2 large eggs
- ½ teaspoons vanilla essence
- ½ teaspoons pure almond essence
- 3 tablespoons canola oil
- 8 tablespoons all-purpose flour
- 1½ teaspoons cornstarch
- 8 tablespoons sugar
- ¼ teaspoons salt
- 3 teaspoons water

HHHHHHHHHHHHHHHHHHHHHHHHHHHHHHHHHHHHHH

Instructions:

1. First of all, prepare strips of paper 3½" long x ½" wide. With a fine nib pen, write fortune messages on the strips.

2. Lightly grease a 13x9" cookie sheet.

3. In a mixing bowl, light beat the egg white together with the essences and canola oil until frothy but not at all stiff.

4. In a second bowl, sift in the flour followed by the cornstarch, sugar, and salt. Add the water and stir.

5. Add the flour mixture to the egg white mixture and stir well to form a batter that is smooth and drops fairly easily off a wooden spoon, without being runny.

6. Spoon level tablespoons of batter onto the cookie sheet, placing them approximately 3" apart. Very gently tilt the cookie sheet from side to side, and back and forth so that each mound of batter becomes a 4" circle.

7. Bake for 12-15 minutes, or until the rims of the cookies are golden and they can be easily removed from the cookie sheet, using a fish slice or spatula.

8. Working very speedily, remove the cookies from the sheet and flip over in your hand.

9. Carefully put a piece of fortune paper into the center of each cookie. Fold the cookie in half, to make a fortune cookie shape, and gently pull the edges downwards over the rim of a glass.

10. Transfer the cookie to a muffin tin cup so that it retains its shape.

11. Repeat until all of the cookies are assembled.

Recipe 38: Chinese Egg Tarts

A Hong Kong classic, these tiny tarts can be found in bakeries, coffee shops and dim sum carts all over Asia.

Makes: 10-12

Preparation Time: 15mins

Cook Time: 30mins

Total Cook Time: 45mins

Ingredient List:

- 3 cups all-purpose flour
- 1 teaspoon salt
- 1 cup vegetable shortening
- 4 -6 tablespoons hot tap water
- 3 medium eggs
- ⅓ cup sugar
- 1½ cups milk

HHHHHHHHHHHHHHHHHHHHHHHHHHHHHHHHHHHHH

Instructions:

1. Preheat the main oven to 360 degrees F.

2. In a mixing bowl, add the flour and stir in ½ teaspoons of salt. Add the shortening and mix well to combine, until you achieve a crumbly consistency.

3. Add sufficient water to turn the mixture into dough, form a ball and cut in half.

4. Turn the dough out onto a clean, lightly floured work surface, and roll out to around ⅛" thick.

5. Cut the dough into 12 (2") circles.

6. Arrange the pastry circles into a 12-cup muffin pan, trimming the sides to fill the cups.

7. Add the eggs, sugar and remaining salt in another bowl, and stir. Pour in the milk. Add approximately 2 tablespoons of this mixture into each pastry cup.

8. Bake in the oven for 25-30 minutes.

9. It is important to test that the egg custards are set; you can do this by inserting a tester into the middle of the custard. If the tester comes out clean, the tarts are sufficiently cooked.

10. Allow to cool and serve.

Recipe 39: Eight-Treasure Rice Pudding

This popular Chinese New Year dessert gets its name from the tradition of decorating with 8 varieties of nuts, fruit, and candy.

Makes: 6

Preparation Time: 15mins

Cook Time: 5mins

Total Cook Time: 20mins

Ingredient List:

- ½ cup mango (peeled, chopped)
- ¼ cup seedless green grapes (halved)
- ¼ cup raisins
- ¼ cup dried pineapple (chopped)
- ¼ cup tart, dried cherries
- Nonstick spray
- ¼ teaspoons salt
- 3 cups cooked glutinous rice (hot, divided)
- ¼ cup almond butter
- ¼ cup maple syrup (divided)
- 4 cups water
- 1 tablespoon almonds (chopped)

HHHHHHHHHHHHHHHHHHHHHHHHHHHHHHHHHHHH

Instructions:

1. In a large bowl combine the mango, grapes, raisins, pineapple, and cherries. Spoon ½ of the fruit mixture into an 8" glass bowl, lightly spritzed with nonstick spray.

2. In a bowl, sprinkle the salt over the rice, and toss to combine evenly.

3. Spread half of the rice mixture over the mixed fruit mixture, using a spatula to firmly pack it down.

4. Spread the almond butter over the rice and drizzle with 2 tablespoons maple syrup. Spoon the remaining the fruit mixture over the top.

5. Finally, spread the remaining rice mixture over the fruit mixture, once more using a spatula to pack it down. Drizzle with 2 tablespoons maple syrup.

6. Place a small vegetable steamer, upside down inside a deep, large wok.

7. Add 4 cups of water and simmer.

8. Wearing oven gloves, place the bowl on top of inverted steam.

9. Cover and cook until heated through; this will take 5 minutes.

10. Still wearing gloves, remove the bowl from the wok.

11. Put a plate on top of the bowl, and invert onto a serving plate.

12. Garnish with chopped almonds and serve.

Recipe 40: Earl Grey Tea Infused Mooncake with Duck Eggs

The Chinese New Year centers around the lunar calendar, and this is what makes mooncake so popular at this time of year.

Makes: 10

Preparation Time: 1hour 30mins

Cook Time: 2hours 30mins

Total Cook Time: 4hours

Ingredient List:

- 6 ounces dried lotus seeds (soaked overnight in 2 cups water, drained)
- 3 cups water
- ½ cup sugar
- ¼ cup vegetable oil
- 2 tablespoons strongly brewed Earl Grey tea

Syrup:

- ½ cup sugar
- ½ cup water
- 1 teaspoon baking soda
- 1½ cup all purpose flour
- 2 tablespoons vegetable oil
- 4 cooked salted duck egg yolks
- ¼ cup toasted pine nuts
- 1 egg (beaten)

HHHHHHHHHHHHHHHHHHHHHHHHHHHHHHHHHHHHH

Instructions:

1. Add the lotus seeds to a pan along with 3 cups of water. Bring to boil on low heat, for 60 minutes. Allow to cool for 15 minutes, then transfer the mixture to a blender. Blitz until pasty. Set aside,

2. Add the sugar, together with the vegetable and Earl Grey tea to a clean blender jug. Pulse until combined then strain into a jug. Set to one side.

3. Pour the lotus seed paste into a wok, and while constantly stirring cook the paste over low heat, taking care not to burn. Continue cooking for approximately 20 minutes until the paste thickens. Set to one side to cool.

4. In the meantime, while the paste filling cools, prepare the dough. Over moderate heat, boil the sugar along with ¼ cup of water, constantly stirring until the sugar caramelizes. Pour in the remaining water to dissolve the caramel into syrup. Mix in the baking soda, flour, and vegetable oil until combined. Set to one side.

5. Next, prepare the eggs. Take a sharp knife and carefully slice the shell all the way around. Scoop the egg yolks out from the cooked salted duck eggs without cutting through or

breaking the yolks. Use a small spoon to scoop the yolk out and clean off the egg white.

6. Preheat the main oven to 350 degrees F.

7. When you are ready to prepare the mooncake, combine the pine nuts with the set-aside cooked lotus seed paste to make the filling. Separate the filling and prepared dough into 4 equal-sized portions.

8. Using your right thumb and left palm shape each filling portion into a deep bowl shape. Drop an egg into the middle and roll the filling into a ball.

9. Mold each dough portion into a slightly bigger bowl and place the filling inside.

10. Gently mold the dough to seal in the filling. Now, roll the cake into a ball.

11. Flour the cake generously and place inside the mooncake mold. Press firmly downwards. Flip the mold over and rap it to loosen the cake.

12. Bake the cakes in the oven for 15 minutes.

13. Take out of the oven and lightly brush the cakes with beaten egg.

14. Pop back in the oven and bake for another 10 minutes.

15. Allow to cool.

About the Author

Angel Burns learned to cook when she worked in the local seafood restaurant near her home in Hyannis Port in Massachusetts as a teenager. The head chef took Angel under his wing and taught the young woman the tricks of the trade for cooking seafood. The skills she had learned at a young age helped her get accepted into Boston University's Culinary Program where she also minored in business administration.

Summers off from school meant working at the same restaurant but when Angel's mentor and friend retired as head chef, she took over after graduation and created classic and new dishes that delighted the diners. The restaurant flourished under Angel's culinary creativity and one customer developed more than an appreciation for Angel's food. Several months after taking over the position, the young woman met her future husband at work and they have been inseparable ever since. They still live in Hyannis Port with their two children and a cocker spaniel named Buddy.

Angel Burns turned her passion for cooking and her business acumen into a thriving e-book business. She has authored several successful books on cooking different types of dishes using simple ingredients for novices and experienced chefs alike. She is still head chef in Hyannis Port and says she will probably never leave!

Author's Afterthoughts

With so many books out there to choose from, I want to thank you for choosing this one and taking precious time out of your life to buy and read my work. Readers like you are the reason I take such passion in creating these books.

It is with gratitude and humility that I express how honored I am to become a part of your life and I hope that you take the same pleasure in reading this book as I did in writing it.

Can I ask one small favour? I ask that you write an honest and open review on Amazon of what you thought of the book. This will help other readers make an informed choice on whether to buy this book.

My sincerest thanks,

Angel Burns

If you want to be the first to know about news, new books, events and giveaways, subscribe to my newsletter by clicking the link below

https://angel-burns.gr8.com

or Scan QR-code